Everyday Home-style Cooking
50 Great Recipes

£1.50

CW01045288

Author: Kevin Cordeiro

Table of Contents

Introduction

Dear Reader,   Thank you for purchasing Everyday Portuguese Home-style Cooking. I love to cook and make the most delicious food possible. This book has a collection of fifty delicious recipes.

It was a joy to fill the pages of this book with recipes that offer some authentic Portuguese dishes, as well as some traditional American favorites prepared using ingredients and flavors of Portugal. I hope you love these recipes as much as I do.

All the best!
Sincerely, Kevin M. Cordeiro
Web Page: www.everydayportuguese.com

Follow me on Facebook: www.facebook.com/kevinmcordeiro

Portuguese Sausage

Many of the recipes include Chourico, a Portuguese sausage. Depending on what is available in your region other types of sausage can be substituted.

Portuguese chouriço: is made with pork, fat, wine, paprika and salt. It is then stuffed into natural or artificial casings and slowly dried over smoke. There are many different varieties, differing in color, shape, seasoning and taste. Many dishes of Portuguese cuisine and Brazilian cuisine make use of chouriço.

A popular way to prepare chouriço is partially sliced and flame-cooked over alcohol at the table. Special glazed earthenware dishes with a lattice top are used for this purpose.

Linguiça: can be found mostly at Brazilian or Portuguese restaurants in Mexico, or where there are significant Brazilian immigrants. In Brazil, the linguiça refers to meat sausages. Linguiça (Portuguese pronunciation: [lĩn gwee sa]) is a form of smoke cured pork sausage seasoned with garlic and paprika in Portuguese-speaking countries.

Linguica's popularity compares with pepperoni in the United States. Thus it's common to differentiate linguiça prepared from the original Portuguese recipe. It's also served on pizzas as mild sausage.

In Hawaii, McDonald's restaurants serve breakfasts featuring linguiça. Hawaiian linguiça, also known as Portuguese sausage, is usually smoked using banana leaves.

Spanish chorizo: is made from coarsely chopped pork and pork fat, seasoned with smoked pimentón (paprika) and salt. It is generally classed as either picante (spicy) or dulce (sweet), depending upon the type of smoked paprika used. Hundreds of regional varieties of Spanish chorizo, both smoked and unsmoked, may contain garlic, herbs and other ingredients

Chorizo comes in short, long, hard and soft varieties; the leaner varieties are suited to being eaten at room temperature as an appetizer or tapas, whereas the fattier versions are generally used for cooking.

Appetizers

Portuguese Potato Skins page 14

Portuguese Egg Rolls

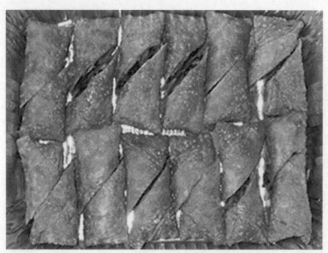

12 Egg Rolls

Ingredients:
4 tablespoons minced red bell pepper
1 tablespoon chopped green onions
1 link chourico (diced into tiny small pieces)
½ cup of chopped frozen spinach
2 pickled jalapeno peppers* (diced)
1 teaspoon parsley
¼ teaspoon garlic powder
¼ teaspoon onion powder
½ teaspoons ground cumin
½ teaspoon chili powder
¾ cup shredded, Monterey jack cheese
¼ cup black beans
Egg wash (2 eggs and 2 tablespoons of water, beat well)
24 egg roll wrappers
Oil for frying
Wax paper

Directions:
1. Mix together the first 11 ingredients in a bowl.
2. Slowly mix in black beans trying not to smash them.
3. You will use 2 wrappers for each egg roll. Layout one egg roll wrapper according to the package instructions.
4. Brush all 4 edges with egg wash. Lay second wrapper on top of the first one and do the same thing, brush all 4 edges with egg wash.
5. Add ¼ cup of filling, being sure not to get too close to the edges of wrapper.
6. Follow directions on back of egg roll wrappers on instructions on how to fold and roll an egg roll.
7. Continue stuffing and rolling all wrappers putting them on wax paper till you have 12 eggrolls.
8. You can freeze them on wax paper for about a half hour for them to set and then fry.
9. You can fry in a deep fryer at 375 degrees or stove top fry in a big enough pan to hold 3 inches of oil on medium high heat.
10. Fry for 10 minutes. Cool and cut in half on a diagonal.

* I use Goya's Green Pickled Jalapeno Peppers for the 2 pickled jalapeno peppers

Portuguese Calzone Roll

Ingredients:
1 package frozen spinach (defrosted)
1 link of chourico
2 tablespoons olive oil
½ teaspoon salt
¼ teaspoon black pepper
¼ teaspoon garlic powder
¼ teaspoon onion powder
¼ cup grated parmesan cheese
1 can of large whole black olives, pitted
1 package of 5 cheese blend (like - Kraft Natural Shredded Cheese, Five Cheese)
1 beaten egg
Dough (store bought fresh at your local grocery)

Directions:
1. Preheat oven to 350
2. Add oil to skillet and heat over medium high heat. Add spinach and sauté for 5 minutes.
3. Add the salt, black pepper, onion and garlic powder.
4. Stir and cook for about 15 more minutes till the moister from the spinach is evaporated.
5. Sprinkle a little flour on a dry surface.
6. Roll out dough on a floured surface into a large rectangle shape; sprinkle the parmesan cheese over the top of dough.
7. Make sure all the following ingredients going on the dough are kept about an inch away from the edges of the dough.
8. Add cooked spinach on top of the dough.
9. Slice the chourico into thin slices and add throughout the top of the dough.
10. Slice 10 of the large olives and add on top of dough.
11. Sprinkle 1 cup of the 5 cheese blend over dough.
12. Brush the sides of the dough with the beaten egg.
13. Roll dough up and tuck the sides under and place on greased baking sheet.
14. With a knife put 3 small slices into the top of the rolled dough.
15. Bake for 1 hour

Let cool for about ½ hour and slice.

Tip – I lay the dough out on a large piece of aluminum foil. This makes it much easier to roll by lifting the foil as you fold.

Portuguese Stuffed Jalapenos

Ingredients:
8 fresh jalapeno peppers, *cut lengthwise
1 link chourico, skin removed and chopped
6 ounces cream cheese, softened
1 cup grated Monterey Jack cheese
¼ teaspoon cayenne pepper
2 large eggs
2 tablespoons milk
½ cup panko crumbs
½ cup fine dry breadcrumbs
½ cup all-purpose flour

Spice Mix
1 ½ teaspoon salt
1 ½ teaspoon paprika
1 ½ teaspoon black pepper
¾ teaspoon garlic powder
¾ teaspoon onion powder

Directions:

1. Preheat the oven to 350 degrees F. Lightly grease a baking sheet and set aside.
2. Mix spice mix ingredients together and set aside.
3. In a bowl, cream together, cream cheese, Monterey jack cheese and cayenne pepper. Then add chourico, mix together.
4. In another small bowl, beat together the eggs, milk, 2 teaspoons of spice mix.
5. In a shallow dish, combine the bread crumbs and another 2 teaspoons of spice mix.
6. In a second shallow dish, combine the flour and remaining 2 teaspoons of spice mix.
7. Spread 2 tablespoons of the cheese mixture into each whole jalapeno.
8. Close jalapeno pepper back to the shape and look of a whole pepper.
9. Do the following coating process TWICE for each whole pepper.
10. One at a time, dredge in the flour, then dip into the egg mixture and then dredge in the bread crumbs, pressing to coat, repeat.
11. Place the coated peppers on the baking sheet and bake until the crust is golden, about 30 minutes.

* Cut jalapeno peppers lengthwise, almost in half; be sure not to cut completely in half, leave stem connected.
Carefully remove seeds and membranes in each jalapeno pepper.

Portuguese Potato Skins

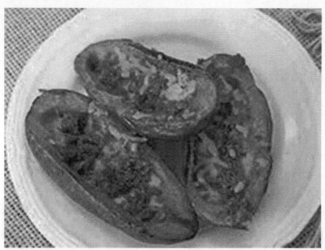

This potato is a crispy tasty delight. Stuffed with linguica and cheese, it makes an easy hot appetizer to enjoy right out of the oven or at room temperature.
Serves 6

Ingredients:
4 medium russet potatoes
1 tablespoon snipped fresh chives
¼ cup butter, melted
1 ½ cups shredded cheddar cheese
½ cup ground linguica

Directions:

1. Poke potatoes with a fork on both sides. This will prevent them from bursting in microwave.
2. Microwave potatoes for 6 minutes. Turn over potatoes and microwave for another 6 minutes.
3. Cook a little longer if potatoes are not fully cooked. Potatoes should be soft.
4. When the potatoes are cool enough to handle, make 2 length-wise cuts through each potato. Resulting in three 1/2-inch slices per potato (the 2 skin ends and the middle). Discard the middle slice or save them for a separate dish of mashed potatoes. This will leave you with two potato skins per potato that are not too deep. (see image below)
5. With a spoon, scoop some of the potato out of each skin, being sure to leave about ¼ inch of potato inside of the skin.
6. Brush the entire surface of each potato skin, inside and outside, with the melted butter.
7. Place the skins on a cookie sheet, cut side up, and broil them for 6 to 8 minutes or until the edges begin to turn dark brown.
8. Sprinkle 2 to 3 tablespoons of Cheddar cheese into each skin.
9. Sprinkle the ground linguica onto the cheese.
10. Broil the skins for 2 more minutes or until the cheese is thoroughly melted. Serve hot

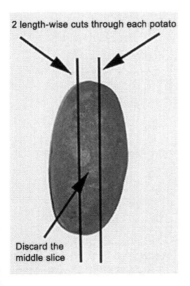

2 length-wise cuts through each potato

Discard the middle slice

Portuguese Deviled Eggs

Makes 16 Deviled Eggs

Ingredients:
8 boiled eggs peeled
2 tablespoon finely chopped onion
1 tablespoon butter
1 tablespoon olive oil
1 teaspoon minced garlic
½ cup of ground linguica or chourico
1 teaspoon of tomato sauce
1 pinch of black pepper
1 pinch of dried parsley
½ cup of mozzarella cheese, plus another ½ cup

Directions:
1. Cut boiled eggs in half lengthwise.
2. Using a teaspoon remove the yolks carefully and add to a bowl.
3. Mash the yolks with a fork, set aside.
4. Heat a sauté pan over medium heat. Add olive oil, butter, onion and garlic.
5. When the onion is translucent, add the sausage, tomato sauce, pepper and parsley.
6. Stir and sauté for about 5 minutes.
7. Remove from heat and add to the bowl of mashed egg yolks and mix in ½ cup of the cheese.
8. With a tablespoon fill the egg whites.
9. Arrange them on a greased baking dish, sprinkle with the other ½ cup of cheese on the top of each deviled egg.
10. Broil till top cheese is melted.

Cheese Bread Bowl

A simple and delicious recipe that's easy to make and always a hit.

Ingredients:
2 mini French boule or 2 large crusty hard rolls
¼ cup of ground linguica or chourico
1 can of Campbell's cheddar cheese condensed soup
¼ cup milk
2 teaspoons of mayonnaise
¼ teaspoon dried parsley
½ cup mozzarella cheese
¼ of an onion
1 pinch of cayenne pepper

Directions:
1. Preheat oven to 425
2. Cut the tops of the rolls. Empty the inside of bread bowl and toast the tops (cover for the bread bowl)
3. In a blender or food processor, blend the soup, milk and onion, blend well until a puree texture.
4. Add this mixture to a sauce pan and bring to a simmer.
5. Add the linguica or chourico, mayonnaise, parsley, salt and pepper.
6. Cook for 10 minutes stirring often so not to stick to pan.
7. Remove from heat and pour into bread bowls
8. Add ¼ cup of mozzarella cheese on top of each bread bowl on the soup.
9. Bake for about 15 minutes or until the cheese is bubbly.
10. Remove from oven and serve immediately with the toasted top to cover.

Marinated Mushrooms

Ingredients:
8 oz of your favorite fresh mushrooms
1 package of Good Seasons Italian all Natural Salad Dressing Mix
¼ cup of balsamic vinegar
¼ cup water
¼ cup olive oil
¼ cup canola oil

Directions:
1. Blend vinegar, water and good season mix. Mix vigorously till well blended.
2. Add the oils and mix vigorously till well blended.
3. Add mushrooms to a bowl or jars and pour marinade over mushrooms and mix together.
4. Cover and store in fridge overnight.

Beef and Pork

Portuguese Pot Roast page 36

Crockpot Cacoila

This is a tender Portuguese stewed pork and beef. It is cooked in a rich, flavorful red wine sauce. Soooooo good!
Serves 6

Ingredients:
1 lb beef; cut into cube pieces (any less expensive steak or stew beef)
1 lb pork meat, cut into cube pieces
1 link of chourico, skin removed cut into 1 inch pieces (optional)
2 medium onions (chopped)
1 teaspoon crushed garlic
1 teaspoons hot crushed red pepper flakes
½ tablespoon salt
½ tablespoon paprika
½ teaspoon black pepper
1 teaspoon allspice
1 bay leaf
1 tablespoons Bacon Fat* or Crisco
½ cup red wine**
½ a can of an 8oz can of tomato sauce.

Directions:

1. Mix all ingredients together in crock-pot. Cook for 5 hours on high or 8 hours on low. When done meat should be very tender.
2. Remove bay leaves.
3. Break meat apart and mash and mix well. You will notice in the beginning there will be a lot of liquid, but as you shred and mash meat and break apart, it will get to a pulled pork consistency.

* *"When I cook bacon, I always save the drippings and freeze. Bacon fat adds flavor to this recipe."*

** *"I use a Portuguese wine like Port wine, but you can use any red wine."*

Left overs can be frozen and make another meal or quick lunch.

Crockpot Brazilian Feijoada

A rich black bean stew with pork, beef and sausage.

Ingredients:
1 large onion cut into quarters
½ lb bacon diced
2 links of chourico, skin removed and cut into bite size pieces
1 lb of beef for stew
1 lb of boneless pork cutlets cut into cubes
1 tablespoon of crushed garlic
1 teaspoon salt
½ teaspoon ground coriander
½ teaspoon black pepper
1 bay leaf
1 tablespoon olive oil
1 cup white wine
2 cans black beans with their juices

Directions:
1. Mix in all above ingredients to a crockpot except black beans.
2. Cook on high for 4 hours.
3. Add beans and mix in. Cook on high for an additional hour.
4. Remove bay leaf and serve.

Portuguese Chop Suey

A delicious American classic made with chourico. This is a great comfort food.
Serves 6

Ingredients:
2 tablespoons olive oil
1 large onion, chopped
½ of a green pepper, chopped
2 red chili peppers chopped
1 link of chourico, diced
1 lb ground beef
½ cup ketchup
1 cup tomato sauce
2 ½ teaspoons salt
½ teaspoon black pepper
½ teaspoon crushed hot red pepper flakes
1 lb box of elbow macaroni
1 cup hot water
½ cup grated parmesan cheese

Directions:
1. Cook pasta according to package directions. Drain and toss with a little oil to keep it moist. Set aside.
2. Add oil to a large saucepan and heat on medium high heat.
3. Add onion, green pepper and chili peppers. Sauté for 10 minutes.
4. Add chourico and ground beef to pan. Break the ground beef apart. Cook for 10 minutes.
5. Add the water, ketchup, tomato sauce, salt, black pepper and hot pepper. Mix everything together.
6. Simmer and cook for 20 minutes, stir occasionally.
7. Add cooked macaroni and mix well, cook for 10 minutes, stirring occasionally.
8. Add cheese and mix together.

Serve with some crusty bread or garlic bread.

Left overs can be frozen and make another meal or quick lunch.

Slow Cooker Carne de Espeto

A Classic Madeiran Dish. Sirloin tips marinated, grilled, and then slow cooked with onions and wine.
Serves 6

Ingredients:
1 bottle Madeira wine
2 cups water
1 tablespoons paprika
½ teaspoon crushed hot red pepper flakes
½ teaspoon black pepper
2 ½ teaspoons salt
2 tablespoons chopped garlic
3 onions, sliced cut in quarters
1 teaspoon gravy master
1 tablespoon sugar
2 beef bouillon cubes
1 tablespoon vegetable oil
2 packages beef stew meat
6 wooden skewers pre-soaked in water, optional*

Directions:
1. Mix together wine, water, paprika, black pepper, hot pepper, salt and garlic. Marinate the meat overnight.
2. Save marinate, braise meat on medium high in vegetable oil, in small batches. Turn meat and brown on all sides
3. Add marinate to pan and deglaze the pan. Keep stirring and bring to a boil.
4. Add the saved marinate, the onion, bouillon cubes, sugar and braised meat to crockpot and cook on high for 6 hours.

Meat will be so tender it will fall apart. Meat can be served with mashed potatoes or rice. Gravy from crockpot is so delicious. Garnish with parsley.

You can put meat on skewers to make it easier to brown meat on all sides by just turning the skewers, but this is optional. You can still do in small batches without skewers and turn each piece of meat as it browns in the pan.

Beef with Chourico and Fries

Serves 6

Ingredients:
2 lbs ground beef
1 link Chourico sausage, sliced
2 teaspoons crushed garlic
1 tablespoon olive oil
1 teaspoon salt
½ teaspoon pepper
2 teaspoons paprika
2 bay leaves
2 pinches of each herb (basil, marjoram and rosemary)
½ cup Madeira wine
2 cups beef broth
2 packets of Sazon Goya Sin Achiote*
Green olives
½ teaspoon crushed red pepper
1 bag of frozen fries

Directions:

1. Brown beef in olive oil, then drain. Return to pan.
2. Add sliced chourico and sauté 10 min
3. Add all other ingredients except green olives and fries and mix. Cook for 10 min.
4. Cook fries, follow instructions on the bag.
5. Mix in cooked fries and green olives.

* Sazon Goya Sin Achiote (without Annatto)

Marinated Pork (Bifanas)

Ingredients:
2 lbs boneless pork, cut evenly about a 1/4 inch thick
2 teaspoons crushed garlic
2 bay Leafs
1 ½ teaspoons salt
½ teaspoon black pepper
1 tablespoon paprika
1 teaspoon sugar
½ teaspoon crushed red pepper
1 ½ cup white wine
½ teaspoon garlic powder
½ teaspoon onion powder

Directions:
1. Put all ingredients in a bowl except pork and mix well.
2. Add the pork to the bowl and Marinate overnight.
3. Grill pork and serve as a sandwich or with rice.

Portuguese Pot Roast

Slow cooked right in your crock-pot

Ingredients:
3-pound bottom round or rump roast, strings removed
3 cups dry red wine
6-ounce can tomato paste
½ tablespoon dried parsley
½ teaspoon oregano
2 bay leaves
2 tablespoons paprika
½ teaspoons crushed red-hot pepper flakes
2 teaspoons salt
2 teaspoons sugar
3 tablespoons crushed garlic
2 links chouriço casing removed
3 onions, sliced then cut into quarters
1 cup water
6 medium Yukon Gold potatoes, peeled and quartered
6 medium carrots, peeled and cut in half
1 Tablespoon olive oil
¼ pound lean bacon

Directions:
1. Sauté the bacon in the olive oil until drippings are rendered and bacon is browned a bit and crisp; transfer bacon to a paper towel-lined plate to drain. Snack on the bacon while you complete the recipe.
2. In the bacon drippings, brown the beef roast well on all sides over moderately high heat.
3. In a medium mixing bowl, whisk the wine and tomato paste until smooth.
4. Stir in sugar, herbs, spices and salt. Set aside.
5. Place browned beef and chouriço in crockpot. Evenly distribute garlic and onions, potatoes and carrots around meat. Pour in wine mixture.
6. Cook in crock-pot on high heat for 8 hours.

Slow-Cooked Pork Loin

Cook in your crock-pot in a delicious hot and spicy garlic sauce.

Ingredients:
4 pound pork loin roast, bone-in
4 cups of beef broth
2 tablespoons minced garlic
1 medium onion, sliced
½ pound red chili peppers, seeds removed and sliced
2 tablespoons butter
½ teaspoon black ground pepper
1 teaspoon salt
1 teaspoon sugar
1 tablespoons paprika
½ cup white wine
½ cup red wine

Directions:
Add all the ingredients to your crockpot and cook on high for 8 hours.

Portuguese Meatloaf

Ingredients:
1 ½ lbs ground beef
1 pound ground chourico
1 beaten egg
1 small onion, chopped
2 teaspoons crushed garlic
¼ teaspoon of oregano
1 teaspoon salt
½ teaspoon black pepper
½ cup plain breadcrumbs plus ¼ cup
2 tablespoons red wine
Olive oil
4 boiled eggs

Directions:
1. Preheat oven to 350 F.
2. Mix the ground meat, chourico , garlic and onion.
3. Add the egg, salt, oregano, pepper and wine, mix well.
4. Add the ½ cup of breadcrumbs in order to give consistency to the meat and mix in well.
5. Grease a sheet of aluminum foil with butter and sprinkle with remaining ¼ cup of breadcrumbs over the butter.
6. Spread the meat on the foil to form a rectangle. Overlap boiled eggs and roll, with the help of the foil.
7. Place the roll in a pan, remove the foil and baste meat loaf with olive oil and red wine.
8. Cover with aluminum foil and bake about 50 minutes.
9. Halfway through the baking remove foil so the meatloaf can brown, basting from the dripping at the bottom of pan.
10. Cut the meat into slices and serve.

Chourico, Peppers, Onions & Potatoes

Sausage roasted with onions, peppers and potatoes. Make with Chourico or Italian sausage.
Serves 8

Ingredients:
2 green bell peppers, seeded and sliced
2 red bell peppers, seeded and sliced
4 medium onions sliced
8 red skin potatoes cut up into quarters
4 Links of chourico or Italian sausage, sliced
2 teaspoons crushed garlic
1 teaspoon salt
¼ teaspoon crushed red pepper flakes
½ teaspoon black pepper
2 tablespoons of olive oil
¼ cup seasoned dry bread crumbs

Directions:
1. Preheat oven to 400
2. Mix all ingredients together.
3. Bake for 1½ hours. Mix every ½ hour so most of the sides of potatoes and sausage brown.

Portuguese Spaghetti

I bet you envision a spaghetti dish full with tomato sauce. This dish is light on the tomato sauce with, ground beef and chourico.
An exceptional tasting dish.
Serves 8

Ingredients:
2 large onions, sliced and cut into quarters
2 tablespoons of olive oil
2 tablespoons minced garlic
1 pound ground beef
1 pound ground chourico
1 teaspoon salt
½ teaspoon black pepper
1 28oz can crushed tomatoes, ground peeled (Chunky Style)
¼ cup soy sauce
½ teaspoon dry basil
1 pound spaghetti, cooked in water

Directions:

1. Cook pasta according to package directions. Drain and toss with a little oil to keep it moist. Set aside.
2. In a large skillet, over medium-high heat add olive oil and sauté onions and garlic until translucent, about 10 minutes.
3. Add the ground meats, salt and pepper and sauté until browned, about 10 minutes.
4. Add the crushed tomato, soy sauce and basil and bring to a simmer.
5. Simmer for an hour stirring occasionally.
6. Combine spaghetti with sauce in pasta pot, and serve.

Left overs can be frozen and make another meal or quick lunch.

Portuguese Stuffed Zucchini

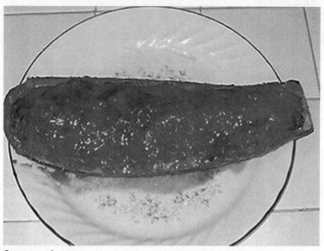

Serves 4

Ingredients:
1 large zucchini
½ pound of ground beef
½ pound ground chourico
1 small onion diced
1 teaspoon crushed garlic
1 teaspoon salt
½ teaspoon black pepper
1 egg beaten
½ cup bread crumbs
1/3 cup grated parmesan cheese
1 jar of pasta sauce
1 can condensed tomato soup

Directions:
1. Preheat oven to 400 F.
2. Cut Zucchini in half lengthwise and then scoop out the seeds and some of the flesh out making two small zucchini boats.
3. Mix can of condensed tomato soup with 1 can of water and add to bottom of casserole oven dish.
4. Add onion and garlic and mix it into the ground meats along with the seasonings and beaten egg, mix well.
5. Add bread crumbs and parmesan cheese, mix again.
6. Add a handful of the meat mixture and put it into the zucchinis you have cleaned out.
7. Place it skin side down and filling side up into your casserole dish.
8. Cover tightly with foil and place in oven. Let it cook for 30 minutes.
9. Remove the foil and add jar of pasta sauce over zucchini boats.
10. Bake an additional 15 minutes, uncovered.
11. Cut the zucchini into slices and serve.
12. The sauce on the bottom of the pan makes a delicious gravy over the zucchini.

Easy Portuguese Chili

Hope you like it HOT! Hot Stuff that is!
To keep this Chili recipe from turning out too greasy, I cook the ground
beef first; cook only till the pink is gone. Also, to keep the recipe's
beans from turning mushy and breaking apart, I add them during the
last hour of cooking.

Ingredients:
1 lb ground beef
1 lb ground chourico
1/3 cup chili powder
1 tablespoon cumin powder
1 teaspoon dried minced onion
1 teaspoon dried minced garlic
1 teaspoon salt
1 ½ teaspoon paprika
Cayenne Pepper (optional) mild ½ teaspoon - medium ¾ teaspoon –
hot 1 ¼ teaspoon
8 oz can tomato sauce
8 oz can of water
1 can of dark kidney beans, with juices
1 can black beans, with juices
1 can pinto beans, with juices

Directions:
1. Brown ground beef, drain and add to crockpot.
2. Add all other ingredients and mix well.
3. Cook on high for 5 hours

Left overs can be frozen and make another meal or quick lunch.

Chicken

Chicken and Broccoli page 56

Chicken Madeira

Sautéed chunks of boneless chicken in a savory sauce of mushrooms, garlic and Madeira wine.
Serves 4

Ingredients:
2 pounds boneless, skinless chicken
2 cups Wondra Flour (Cake Flour)
4 teaspoons salt
4 teaspoons oregano
4 tablespoons olive oil
4 tablespoons butter
1 large onion, sliced cut into quarters.
1 teaspoon black pepper
2 package of sliced mushrooms
1 cup Madeira wine (usually found at your local liquor store)
2 cups chicken broth mixed with 1 teaspoon chopped garlic

Directions:

1. Pound chicken breasts between sheets of "Saran Wrap" until about ¼ inch even-thickness cut into 3 inch pieces.
2. Combine flour, salt, pepper and oregano, blend.
3. Dredge chicken pieces in the flour, shake off excess.
4. Heat oil and butter in frying pan over medium heat. Add onion and sauté for about 5 minutes.
5. Add the dredged chicken and cook the breasts for about four minutes on the first side, until lightly brown.
6. Turn chicken pieces over to second side to cook, add the mushrooms around and on top of the chicken pieces
7. Cook chicken about four more minutes, until lightly browned on the second side, stir the mushrooms.
8. When chicken is browned, add Madeira wine and chicken broth. Mix around the chicken and mushrooms, cover and simmer for about 20 minutes.

Garnish with parsley and serve with white rice or your favorite pasta.

Portuguese Chicken and Rice

Serves 6

Ingredients:
1 ½ lbs boneless chicken breast cut into strips
2 links of chourico or chorizo (Portuguese or Spanish sausage) sliced
2 tablespoons olive oil
1 small green bell pepper, seeded and chopped
1 large onion, diced
½ cup red wine
1 tablespoon crushed garlic
2 teaspoons salt
½ teaspoon black pepper
¼ teaspoon hot crushed red pepper flakes
1 (8 ounce) can tomato sauce
1½ cups chicken stock
1½ cups 5 minute white rice
½ cup pimientos, chopped

Directions:
1. Heat oil in large pan over medium heat. Add onion and green pepper and sauté for about 10 minutes.
2. Move onions and peppers off to the sides of the pan. Raise heat to medium high and add chicken, season by adding the salt, black pepper and pepper flakes. Lightly cook both sides of chicken.
3. Add chourico and mix everything together, cook for 10 minutes
4. Add wine and deglaze pan stirring everything in pan together.
5. Add chicken stock, garlic, tomato sauce and pimiento. Bring to a boil.
6. Add rice and stir together and bring back to boil.
7. Once back up to a boil, cover and shut heat off and let sit for 10 minutes.

Chicken and Broccoli

I've seen and tried many of these similar casseroles, but somehow none of them quite match the flavor of this one!
Serves 6

Ingredients:
1 ½ lbs. chicken breast
3 tablespoons olive oil
½ lb of your favorite pasta
1 ½ cups heavy whipping cream
3 tablespoons butter
1 teaspoon salt
2 teaspoons minced garlic
2 teaspoons cornstarch
2 bunches broccoli florets, cut into bite size pieces
2 tablespoons grated Parmesan cheese

Spice Mixture:
1 teaspoon each of; dried basil, parsley, and rosemary
½ teaspoon each crushed red pepper flakes, salt, black pepper
¼ teaspoon onion powder

Directions:

1. Combine ingredients from spice mixture. Rub onto the chicken breasts.
2. Cook chicken in the olive oil till done and both sides browned, set aside.
3. Cook pasta and broccoli together in a large pot of boiling ½ teaspoon salted water until pasta is "almost" done. Drain, and return pasta and broccoli to pot.
4. Stir butter, salt and garlic into a large sauté pan over medium heat. Cook for 5 minutes, and then add the cornstarch till it thickens the sauce.
5. Add the cream then the cooked pasta, mix together.
6. Cut the cooked chicken into desired size pieces and add chicken, and broccoli into the pasta. Mix everything together.
7. Simmer for 10 minutes, and remove from heat.

Sprinkle with Parmesan cheese.

Cranberry Chicken and Rice

Make this effortless, satisfying, one pot dish that has the bold flavor of cranberries.
Serves 6

Ingredients:
6 chicken thighs with skin
1 teaspoon salt
¼ teaspoon black pepper
3 medium onions, sliced thin
1 cup red wine
1 can gelled cranberries with whole cranberries
2 tablespoons minced garlic
2 tablespoons soy sauce
1 tablespoon dark brown sugar
1 teaspoons white vinegar
¼ teaspoon garlic powder
1 ½ cups chicken stock or chicken broth
1 ½ cups 5 minute white rice

Directions:

1. Preheat oven 375 degrees.
2. Place chicken in a large oven proof casserole and season the chicken with the salt and pepper.
3. Place onions on top of chicken.
4. In a large bowl add all other ingredients, except rice, and mix together.
5. Mix till the gelled cranberries are dissolved and pour over chicken and onions.
6. Cook uncovered for 50 minutes.
7. When chicken is done, remove casserole from oven. Let rest for 10 minutes
8. In a sauce pan bring chicken stock to a boil, then add 5 minute rice, stir, cover and take off heat then let rest for 10 minutes.
9. Serve chicken over rice.

Hot and Spicy Fried Chicken

Ingredients:
1 cup all-purpose flour
1 cup corn starch
1 teaspoon Fines Herbs Seasoning Mix*
1 tablespoon paprika
1 teaspoon cayenne pepper
2 teaspoons salt
1 ½ teaspoons black pepper
½ teaspoon garlic powder
½ teaspoon onion powder
1/3 cup whole milk
¼ cup chicken wing sauce **
1 egg
Legs and chicken thighs (9 pieces)
Oil for deep-fat frying

Directions:

1. In a shallow bowl, mix the first nine ingredients.
2. In a separate shallow bowl, whisk the milk, buffalo wing sauce and egg.
3. Heat the oil on medium high heat to 375°.
4. Dip the chicken pieces, one at a time in the flour mixture, then in the milk mixture, then coat again with flour mixture.
5. Put each piece of coated chicken to the side while oil heats.
6. Fry chicken 3 pieces at a time for 9 minutes on each side.

*Fines Herbs Seasoning
Ingredients:
1 Tablespoon dried tarragon
1 Tablespoon dried chervil
1 Tablespoon dried chives
1 Tablespoon dried parsley
Mix together and store in a small container. Good on grilled chicken too.

**This Brand of Chicken Wing Sauce works great in this recipe.

Seafood

Amêijoas à Espanhola page 72

Fish Casserole

Serves 6

Portuguese-style fish casserole. Lean white-fish fillets cooked in olive oil, with red skin potatoes, onions, garlic, peas and pimiento.

Ingredients:
6 red skin potatoes
2 medium size onions cut in ¼ inch thick slices
1 tablespoon of butter, cut into pieces
2 teaspoons dry parsley or 3 tablespoons of fresh minced parsley
1 tablespoon olive oil
1 teaspoon salt
½ teaspoon black pepper
A pinch of dried thyme
1 cup water
1 teaspoon paprika
1 pound fish such as cod, flounder or other lean white fish
2 cups of frozen peas, thawed
½ cup chopped pimiento

Directions:

1. Spread red potatoes and onion slices in a large pan.
2. Add the olive oil and butter on top of potatoes and onions.
3. Add to pan *half* the amount of the following; parsley, salt and the pepper.
4. Add the garlic, paprika and thyme. Pour water over the top and boil.
5. Reduce heat, cover and simmer 15 minutes till potatoes are almost tender.
6. Arrange fish over the potatoes and onions and sprinkle with remaining parsley, salt and pepper. Cover and simmer 10 minutes longer.
7. Add the peas and pimiento, cover and simmer another 5 minutes.

Serve in soup plates or bowls.

Creamy Cod Au Gratin

Serves 6

Ingredients:
1 ½ pounds of fresh cod or other white fish, cut in 8 pieces
1 large onion, sliced thin
5 tbsp. olive oil
1 ½ pounds of white potatoes, peeled and diced.
½ cups water
1 ¾ cup milk
3 tablespoons butter
3 tablespoons flour
½ teaspoon salt
½ teaspoons black pepper
1 ½ cups heavy cream
½ cup shredded cheddar cheese

Directions:
Sauce:
Melt the butter in a saucepan over medium heat and blend in the flour. Then add the milk and cream, heat, stirring constantly until thickened. Blend in the salt and pepper and put aside.

1. Preheat the oven to 375
2. In a large skillet over medium heat, sauté onion in olive oil until soft and golden.
3. Add the water and potatoes and bring to a quick boil then turn heat to low and cover.
4. Cook for 20 minutes then transfer to a baking casserole dish.
5. Lay the fish on top and sprinkle shredded cheddar over the casserole dish.
6. Then pour the sauce over the dish.
7. Bake uncovered for 40 minutes and serve.

Shrimp Mozambique

Serves 6

Spicy shrimp flavored with wine and garlic. Mozambique gained their freedom from Portugal in 1975, many of the foods of Mozambique have roots in Portugal cuisine.

Ingredients:
4 tablespoons butter
3 medium onions, chopped
1 ½ cups water
8 teaspoons crushed garlic
2 tablespoons finely chopped cilantro.
2 packets Sazon Goya, for seafood (con azafran)*
½ cup red wine
2 teaspoons fresh lemon juice
2 teaspoons salt
½ teaspoon ground black pepper
1 tablespoons chili sauce
1 generous pinch crushed red pepper
2 pounds raw shrimp (26-30 count), peeled and deveined
1 ½ cups of white 5 minute rice.

Directions:

1. Melt butter in large pot over medium heat.
2. Toss in onion and sauté for 20 minutes.
3. Pour in the 1 cup of the water followed by garlic, goya, salt and pepper. Cover and simmer for 8 - 10 minutes, allowing the essence of the spices and herbs to mingle.
4. Pour in the wine with the lemon juice, hot pepper, chili sauce and ½ cup of water.
5. Stir. Cover and raise heat to medium-high and bring the sauce to a boil.
6. Toss in the shrimp, white rice and cilantro, mix well. Cover and reduce the heat to medium-low and simmer for 10 minutes.
7. Remove from heat and let rest for 10 minutes.

*Sazon Goya, for seafood (con azafran)

Carne Porco à Alentejana

Pan seared marinated pork chunks combined with a savory wine sauce. Steamed with little necks and smothered with fried potatoes.

Ingredients
2 ½ - 3 lbs boneless pork loin, cut into 1 inch cubes
2 ½ lbs potatoes, peeled and cut into quarters
2 tablespoons vegetable oil
2 tablespoons bacon fat or crisco
1 large onion, chopped
1 teaspoon sugar
2 tablespoon tomato paste
1 tsp parsley
½ cup of water
24 littleneck clams in the shell, scrubbed

Marinade:
1 teaspoon paprika
1 ½ cups dry white wine
¼ teaspoon black pepper
1 teaspoon salt
¼ teaspoon onion powder
1 large bay leaf
3 tsp garlic

Directions:

1. Marinade the pork in a non-metallic bowl in refrigerator overnight.
2. In a large sauce pan, heat oil or bacon fat on medium high heat. Add marinated pork and brown on all sides. Save marinade.
3. Remove pork from pan, and set aside.
4. Deglaze pan with the saved marinade and add the sugar and water to the pan and stir.
5. Add chopped onion. Cook 10 minutes, till onions are translucent.
6. Deep fry or pan fry potatoes at 375 degrees for 12 minutes while onions cook. When potatoes are cooked let drain on paper towels or brown paper bag. Shake a little salt and pepper over cooked potatoes while they cool.
7. Add tomato paste with onion, stir and mix well.
8. Add the browned pork back to the pan and parsley, stir. Bring pan up to a boil, then add clams on top of the pork, distributing them as evenly as possible. Cover and cook about 20 minutes or until clams open.
9. Add cooked potatoes to pan on top of clam, pork and potatoes and serve.

Amêijoas à Espanhola

Littlenecks Spanish Style (Amêijoas à Espanhola)
Another delicious way to eat clams!
Serves 6

Ingredients:
24 cherry stone or littleneck clams
1 link of Portuguese chourico sausage, sliced
2 medium onions, sliced
2 tablespoons crushed garlic
1 bay leaf
2 tablespoons olive oil
2 tablespoons butter
2 teaspoons your favorite hot sauce
28 oz. can crushed tomatoes
4 oz jar of Goya pimientos, sliced
3 peppers, 1 each (green, yellow, orange)
½ cup red wine
2 packets Sazon Goya, for seafood (con azafran)*
1 teaspoon paprika
1 teaspoon salt
½ teaspoon black pepper

Directions:

1. In a large pan, sauté onions in oil and butter over medium heat for 10 minutes.
2. Then add chourico, peppers and garlic. Cook until peppers are soft.
3. Now add the wine, crushed tomatoes, pimientos and bay leaf. Season with salt, pepper, paprika, hot sauce and Sazon. Let simmer for 20 minutes.
4. Discard bay leaf.
5. Bring to a boil then add littlenecks to the pan cover and cook 10 to 15 minutes or until littlenecks open.

*Sazon Goya, for seafood (con azafran)

Easy Lobster Stuffed Ravioli

Homemade x-large ravioli stuffed with fresh lobster meat with a Portuguese style spicy cheese filling. Wonton wrappers make it very easy for the pasta dough.

Ingredients:
Mashed potatoes (3 potatoes, peeled, boiled and mashed)
2 tablespoons olive oil
½ cup chopped onions
2 tablespoons minced green onions
¼ cup diced green bell peppers
2 tablespoons minced garlic
½ cup chunky crushed tomatoes
1 packets Sazon Goya, for seafood (con azafran)*
¼ teaspoon crushed red hot pepper flakes
¼ teaspoon black pepper
½ teaspoon dried parsley
½ cup grated Parmesan cheese
32 wonton wrappers
1 egg, lightly beaten
Meat from 1 boiled lobster

Directions:

1. In a sauté pan, heat the olive oil.
2. Add the onions, green onions, green pepper and garlic. Sauté for 20 minutes.
3. In a bowl add the cooked onion mixture.
4. Stir in the mashed potatoes, tomatoes, goya, red pepper, black pepper, parsley and cheese. Mix well
5. Separate the wonton wrappers until you have 16 one skin wrappers, and brush each with beaten egg.
6. Mound 1 tablespoon of the filling on each of 16 wrappers and add the cooked lobster evenly on top of each filling.
7. Cover with another 16 wrappers. Crimp the edges with a fork.
8. In a pot of boiling salted water, add the ravioli and cook for about 5 minutes.
9. Remove with a slotted spoon. Season with salt and pepper
10. Serve with your favorite marinara sauce.

*Sazon Goya, for seafood (con azafran)

Scallops Portuguese Style

Ingredients:
1 pound bay scallops
2 tablespoons olive oil
1 medium onion, chopped
1 teaspoon crushed garlic
½ teaspoon dried parsley
2 tablespoons tomato paste
1 tablespoon red wine
¼ teaspoon ground black pepper

TOPPING:
4 tablespoons dry plain breadcrumbs
3 tablespoons grated parmesan cheese
1 tablespoon olive oil

Directions:
1. Preheat oven to 375 F
2. Mix together topping ingredients, set aside.
3. Sauté the scallops in 1 tablespoon of the oil in a large skillet over medium high heat 3 to 4 minutes. Just until they begin to color and released their juices.
4. With a slotted spoon lift the scallops to a bowl and set aside.
5. Add the remaining tablespoon of olive oil, onion, garlic and parsley.
6. Sauté 5 minutes until the onions start to get translucent.
7. Turn heat to low and cover for 10 minutes.
8. Blend in tomato paste, wine and pepper also any juices that may have accumulated in the bowl of scallops. Stir and cook 2 minutes.
9. Add the scallops to the pan and toss lightly.
10. Pour the scallop mixture into a casserole dish and scatter the topping over the scallops.
11. Bake uncovered 15 - 20 minutes till bubbly and a touch of brown.

Shrimp Over Mashed Potatoes

Shrimp sautéed in a seasoning combination of garlic, sugar, salt, vinegar and butter, topped over smashed potatoes......so so delicious!
Serves 4

Ingredients:
4 large potatoes
¼ cup balsamic vinegar
¼ cup rice vinegar
1 tablespoon sugar
4 teaspoons soy sauce
2 tablespoons oil
12 large raw shrimp, peeled and deveined
2 tablespoons minced garlic
¼ teaspoon crushed red hot pepper flakes
¼ teaspoon ground ginger
1 medium size onion
1 medium tomato, diced
½ stick butter
1 teaspoon salt
½ teaspoon black pepper

Directions:
1. Poke a few holes in the potatoes and microwave for 10 minutes or until cooked through.
2. Meanwhile, in a bowl combine the vinegars, sugar and soy sauce and stir until the sugar is dissolved. Set aside.
3. On medium high heat, add the oil to the pan and when hot, add the onions, garlic, crushed red hot pepper and ginger. Sauté about 10 minutes.
4. Add the soy sauce mixture you set aside to the pan and simmer until the mixture is reduced by half, about 5 minutes.
5. Add the tomato, and shrimp. Simmer until the shrimp are cooked through, 2 to 3 minutes or until the shrimp turns pink. Add butter, salt and pepper and simmer till butter is melted and stir.
6. Put each potato on a plate and put several slices in the cooked potatoes and smash them down a little.
Top with the shrimp and sauce over the smashed potatoes and serve.

Portuguese Man-of-War

A delicious meal using bacon, chourico, mussels, scallops, shrimp and little necks.

Ingredients:
2 tablespoons olive oil
2 onions cut into quarters
1 link of chourico skin removed and sliced.
½ lb raw bacon diced
1 can (28 ounces) crushed tomatoes
1 tablespoon crushed garlic
1 cup white wine
1 teaspoon pesto
1 teaspoon chili powder
1 teaspoon paprika
½ teaspoon dried parsley
12 mussels
12 littlenecks
12 large shrimp
½ lb bay scallops

Directions:
1. Heat olive oil in a large pan over medium high heat.
2. Add onions, chourico and bacon. Cook for about 10 minutes.
3. Add the crushed tomatoes, wine, garlic, pesto, chili powder, paprika and parsley. Mix together and let come up to a boil.
4. Add all the seafood. Mix everything together.
5. Cover pan and let cook for 10 minutes or till shells of the shellfish open.

Soups & Sides

Portuguese Kale Soup page 86

Green Soup (Caldo Verde)

Serves 4
Native to Portugal's northwest region of Minho, this green soup is made with a kale, potatoes and chourico.

Ingredients:
3 lbs potatoes, peeled and cubed
5 cups water
1 link of chourico, sliced
½ teaspoon salt
2 beef bouillon cubes
1 bunch of kale, shredded (discard stems)
1 tablespoon olive oil

Directions:
1. Add water and potatoes to pan, boil until the potatoes are soft.
2. Blend* the potatoes in the water until smooth. This will thicken the soup broth.
3. Add the shredded kale leaves, chourico and olive oil to pot. Cook for 20 minutes.

I use a blender to blend potatoes then I add it back to the pan.

Portuguese Kale Soup

Serves 5

This is a very flavorful soup. The Chourico gives the broth a really good flavor. Kale soup is a winter wonder. Serve with warm crusty bread. A great next day soup and freezes well.

Ingredients:
½ gallon of water (8 cups)
4 beef bouillon cubes
1 teaspoon of gravy master or kitchen bouquet
1 bunch of kale. Pull leaves of stems and chop, discard stems
2 links of chourico, skin removed and sliced
1 lb of stew meat
½ small head of cabbage, chopped
2 medium onions, chopped
½ tablespoon kosher salt
½ teaspoon black pepper
½ cup red wine
¼ teaspoon garlic powder
1 tablespoon olive oil
1 can dark red kidney beans
1 lbs potatoes peeled and cut into bite size cubes.

Directions:
1. Bring all ingredients to a boil in at least a 12 quart pot, except potatoes and beans.
2. Cover, reduce heat and simmer for 2 hours.
3. Bring back to a boil, and add potatoes and beans.
4. Cook till potatoes are done to your liking

Serve with some Portuguese bread or other crusty bread.

Left overs can be frozen and make another meal or quick lunch.

Easy Chicken Soup

Serves 8

Ingredients:
2 chicken breast cut into pieces
1 tablespoon of olive oil
1 small chopped onion
1 teaspoon crushed garlic
2 potatoes cut into cubes
1 carrot cut into cubes
1 stewed tomato, chopped
½ cup of white long grain rice
1 green onion, chopped
½ teaspoon dried parsley
8 cups water
1 teaspoon salt
½ teaspoon black pepper

Directions:
1. In a large sauce pan, heat olive oil.
2. Add the onion, garlic and chicken and stir-fry until golden brown.
3. Add the potatoes, carrot, tomato, parsley and rice and mix well.
4. Add the water, salt and pepper and cook over medium heat for 40 minutes.

Add green onion, stir and serve.

String Bean Stew

This is a recipe for delicious green beans and tomato with chourico, cooked the traditional Portuguese way. Fresh green beans, tomatoes, herbs and spices are simmered together long enough for the tastes to blend.

Ingredients:
2 links chourico, sliced
2 tablespoons olive oil
1 28oz. can crushed tomatoes
1 ½ teaspoon salt
1 teaspoon sugar
2 cups water
1 lbs of fresh string beans
1 large onion, chopped
2 teaspoons crushed garlic
1 bay leaf
1 teaspoon paprika
½ teaspoon black pepper
5 potatoes, peeled cut into cubes
¼ teaspoon crushed hot red pepper flakes

Directions:

1. Add oil to pot and sauté onion, garlic and chourico for 15 minutes.
2. Add tomato sauce, salt, black pepper, sugar, water, bay leaf, hot red pepper, string beans and paprika. Simmer for 2 hours or till string beans are cook to your liking.
3. When string beans are cooked add potatoes.
4. Simmer till sauce reduced and potatoes are done.

Favas

Traditional Portuguese style fava beans slow simmered in a juicy Portuguese style sauce with onions and chourico.
Serves 8

Ingredients:
2 tablespoons of olive oil
2 tablespoon bacon fat or Crisco
3 large onions – sliced and cut in quarters
3 teaspoons crushed garlic
2 cups of hot water
½ teaspoon of crushed red hot pepper flakes
8 oz can tomato sauce
1 envelope of Sazon Goya Sin Achiote (without Annatto)*
½ tablespoon of dried parsley
½ teaspoon of black pepper
1 tablespoon of paprika
1 teaspoons salt
1 link of chourico cut up into chunks
2 cans fava beans

Directions:

1. Brown onion in olive oil and bacon fat.
2. Add all ingredients except favas, mix together and bring to a boil. Reduce heat and simmer for 40 minutes stirring occasionally.
3. Add fava beans, juice and all and mix in very gently. Raise heat to bring up back to a steady simmer. Simmer for 20 more minutes.
4. Remove from stove.

Serve with some Portuguese bread or other crusty bread.

Left overs can be frozen and make another meal or quick lunch.

* Sazon Goya Sin Achiote (without Annatto)

Sausage Stuffing with Dried Cherries

Tired of serving the same old stuffing? Then try this simple recipe that gets pumped up with just the right amount of Portuguese sausage and dried cherries. The results will be outstanding!

Ingredients:
2 tbsp. butter
1 package of ground Linguiça or Chourico
1 large onion, chopped (about 1 cup)
2 stalks celery, chopped (about 1 cup)
2 ½ cups Chicken Broth
1 cup dried cherries
1 pkg. (14 ounces) Pepperidge Farm Corn Bread Stuffing

Directions:

1. Heat the butter in a 3-quart saucepan over medium heat.
2. Add the onion and celery and cook until onion and celery is tender and soft, stirring occasionally.
3. Add the ground sausage and mix with the cooked onions and celery and cook for 10 minutes.
4. Remove the saucepan from the heat.
5. Stir the broth and cherries in the saucepan.
6. Add the package of corn bread stuffing and mix lightly.
7. Let stuffing cool and spoon stuffing into a turkey before you a ready to cook.

OR spoon the stuffing mixture into a greased 3-quart casserole. Cover the casserole and bake at 350°F for 30 minutes or until the stuffing mixture is hot.

Baked Bean Casserole with Chourico

I have never seen baked beans disappear and receive raves like this before! Sooo good...you won't be disappointed.

Ingredients:
1 link of chourico, skin removed and cut into bite size pieces
1 cup diced onions
1 cans of 28oz B&M Original Baked Beans
1 granny smith apples, peeled, core removed and diced
1 tablespoons of spicy brown mustard
¼ cup brown sugar
½ teaspoon salt
½ lb bacon cut into 1 ½ inch strips

Directions:
1. Preheat oven to 375 F
2. Coat a baking dish with nonstick cooking spray.
3. In a large bowl combine all the ingredients except the bacon and mix well.
4. Pour into the baking dish.
5. Lay the raw bacon strips on top.
6. Cover with foil and bake for 1 hour and 20 minutes.
7. Uncover and broil for 5 minutes to get the bacon more firm.

Breads and Sweets

Pasteis de Nata (Custard Tarts) page 105

Pumpkin Dreams

I love pumpkin dreams all year long. Moist and delicious every time. Everyone asks for the recipe after they've tried them!

Ingredients:
1¾ cups all-purpose flour
2 teaspoons baking powder
½ teaspoon salt
½ teaspoon cinnamon
½ teaspoon nutmeg
½ teaspoon allspice
1/8 teaspoon ground cloves
1/3 cup vegetable oil
½ cup brown sugar
1 egg
1 teaspoon vanilla extract
¾ cup canned pumpkin
½ cup milk

Coating
1 stick unsalted butter, melted
2/3 cup sugar
2 tablespoons cinnamon

Directions:

1. Preheat oven to 350 F and spray mini muffin tins with non-stick cooking spray.
2. Combine flour, baking powder, salt, and spices in a bowl and whisk until combine.
3. In another bowl, mix oil, brown sugar, egg, vanilla, pumpkin, and milk.
4. Pour in flour mixture and mix until just combined.
5. Fill mini muffin tins until almost full and bake 10-12 minutes. Let cool
6. Melt butter in small bowl.
7. Mix sugar and cinnamon in a separate small bowl.
8. After pumpkin dreams have cooled for a few minutes, dip them in the butter and roll them in the sugar mixture.

Portuguese Sweet Bread

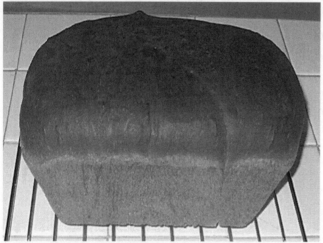

This is a recipe that has been handed down for generations. It is a family favorite bread to have at Easter, but can be made at any time. This recipe makes 1 large loaf. It is very hands-on, requiring kneading but it works very well. Most of the preparation time is the rising.

Dry Ingredients:
2 ½ cups flour
2 teaspoons yeast
1/3 cup plus 1 tablespoon sugar
½ teaspoon salt

Wet Ingredients:
1 egg
½ cup warm milk
3 tablespoons melted unsalted butter
1 ½ teaspoons of vanilla extract
Zest of ½ of lemon

Directions:

1. Mix together your dry ingredients.
2. In another bowl mix together your wet ingredients.
3. Combine wet and dry ingredients together.
4. Mix together the ingredients for 15 minutes
5. Cover and let it double in size for one hour. Punch down dough.
6. Grease large loaf pan.
7. Shape dough more rectangular and add dough to the large loaf pan.
8. Put in warm humid place to let rise for 3 hours.
9. Pre-heat oven to 350F
10. Bake for 30 minutes. You can lay a piece of foil over the top of the bread for the last ten minutes of baking if the top is getting to dark.

Pasteis de Nata (Custard Tarts)

Ingredients:
1 package frozen puff pastry, thawed
1 tablespoon cornstarch
¼ teaspoon vanilla
1 ½ cups heavy cream
1 cup granulated sugar
6 egg yolks

Directions:
1. Preheat oven to 350 degrees F
2. Lightly grease 12 muffin cups and line bottom and sides with puff pastry.
3. Dissolve the cornstarch in a ¼ cup of the cream in a medium bowl, and then add the remaining cream, vanilla and sugar.
4. Stir until the mixture is smooth and the sugar granules are all dissolved; make sure the sugar is stirred till fully dissolved.
5. In a small bowl, blend the yolks until smooth.
6. Add the yolks to the cream mixture, stirring to combine.
7. Add egg mixture into the pastry cups, filling to 2/3 capacity.
8. Bake in at 350°F until crust is golden brown and filling is lightly browned on top about 20 to 25 minutes.

Best Gingerbread Cake

Ingredients:
¾ cup dark stout beer
½ teaspoon baking soda
2/3 cups molasses
¾ cup packed brown sugar
¼ cup granulated sugar
1 ½ cups all-purpose flour, plus extra for dusting pan
2 teaspoons of ground powdered ginger, split in two parts.
½ teaspoon baking powder
½ teaspoon salt
¼ teaspoon ground cinnamon
¼ teaspoon ground black pepper
2 large eggs
1/3 cup vegetable oil

Directions:

1. Adjust oven rack to middle position and heat oven to 350F degrees. Grease and flour 8-inch square baking pan.
2. Bring beer to a boil in a medium saucepan over medium heat, stirring occasionally.
3. Remove from heat and stir in baking soda (mixture will foam vigorously).
4. When foaming subsides, stir in molasses, brown sugar, and granulated sugar until dissolved, set mixture aside.
5. Whisk flour, 1 teaspoon of ground ginger, baking powder, salt, cinnamon, and pepper together in large bowl; set aside.
6. Transfer beer mixture to large bowl. Whisk in eggs, oil and 1 teaspoon of ground ginger.
7. Whisk wet mixture into flour mixture in thirds, mix well stirring vigorously until completely smooth after each addition.
8. Transfer batter to prepared pan and gently tap pan against counter 3 or 4 times to dislodge any large air bubbles.
9. Bake until top of cake is just firm to touch and toothpick inserted into center comes out clean, 35 to 45 minutes.
10. Cool cake in pan on wire rack, about 1 ½ hours.
11. Cut into squares and serve warm or at room temperature.

Easy Apple Pie

This Easy Apple Pie has structure and a delicious taste! By reducing the oven temperature, this will allow the pie to cook longer, giving the apples time to gently soften as the batter sets.

Ingredients:
1 sheet of Pillsbury pie crust
1 stick unsalted butter plus 1 tablespoon, melted
3 Granny Smith apples peeled, cored, quartered, and cut crosswise into thin slices
2 Golden Delicious apples, peeled, cored, quartered, and cut crosswise into thin slices
1 ¼ cups sugar plus 2 tablespoons
1 cup all-purpose flour plus 1 tablespoon
1 ½ teaspoons ground cinnamon
¼ teaspoon ground nutmeg
½ teaspoon baking powder
½ teaspoon salt
2 large eggs, lightly beaten
2 tablespoons sour cream

Directions:

1. Adjust oven rack to middle position and pre-heat oven to 325F degrees.
2. Grease bottom and sides of deep pie plate with 1 tablespoon of butter.
3. Lay in 1 sheet of pie crust pressing bottom and sides. Set pie plate aside.
4. Coat the Apples: In a large bowl toss apples with 2 tablespoons of sugar, and 1 tablespoon of the flour.
5. Add the coated apples to the pie plate.
6. Batter: Combine 1 cup sugar, 1 cup of flour, cinnamon, nutmeg, baking powder, and salt in large bowl.
7. Whisk in eggs, sour cream, and 1 stick of melted butter until smooth.
8. Pour batter evenly over apples.
9. Sprinkle remaining ¼ cup of sugar evenly over batter and bake until deep golden brown and crisp, 70 to 80 minutes.
10. Transfer to wire and cool completely, at least 1 hour.

Chunky Peanut Butter Cookies

Ingredients:
1 ½ cups all-purpose flour
½ teaspoon baking powder
½ teaspoon baking soda
½ teaspoon salt
1 cup chunky peanut butter
1 stick butter, softened
½ cup firmly packed brown sugar
½ cup granulated sugar
1 large egg
½ teaspoon vanilla extract

Directions:
1. Preheat oven to 400 degrees
2. In a medium bowl combine flour, baking powder, baking soda and salt, mix together.
3. In another bowl beat together peanut butter, butter, brown sugar, eggs, vanilla and granulated sugar until smooth.
4. Combine flour mixture with peanut butter mixture, scrapping the sides and making sure batter is well blended.
5. Cover bowl with plastic and place in refrigerator for 30 minutes
6. Using a teaspoon drop the batter 1 inch apart on an ungreased cookie sheet.
7. Using a fork make crisscross pattern flattening cookies slightly.
8. Bake for 10 to 12 minutes

Sauces

Madeira Sauce page 115

Madeira Sauce

A sauce to enhance the flavor of beef, chicken, chops or veal.

Ingredients:
1 medium onion finely chopped
2 tablespoons butter
½ teaspoon of gravy master or kitchen bouquet
½ lb white mushrooms, sliced
½ teaspoon black pepper
1 bay leaf
¼ teaspoon dried thyme
1 cup Madeira wine
1 cup beef stock
¼ cup heavy cream

Directions:
1. In a medium sized saucepan, sauté onions in butter for 5 minutes or until translucent.
2. Add mushrooms, pepper, thyme, and bay leaf cook until mushrooms are tender.
3. Add Madeira wine and bring to boil.
4. Add beef stock and gravy master, whisk until incorporated into the sauce.
5. Add heavy cream and reduce for 5 minutes.

Portuguese Mayonnaise

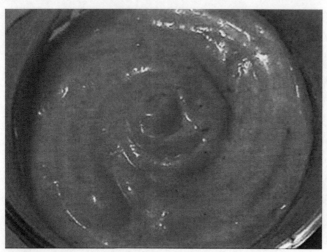

Use as you would any mayonnaise.

Ingredients:
1 ½ teaspoons dry mustard
½ teaspoon salt
¼ teaspoon cayenne pepper
1 tablespoon juice from a lemon
1 tablespoon cider vinegar
2 tablespoons half-and-half cream
2 large egg yolks
1 1/3 cups olive oil

Directions:
1. Place the mustard, salt, cayenne, lemon juice, vinegar, cream and egg yolks in a blender.
2. Pulse several times just to blend the ingredients.
3. Now with the motor running add the olive oil in a very fine stream pausing now and then to scrap the sides down.
4. Continue adding the olive oil until the oil is incorporated.
5. Then continue to let it run nonstop for 30 seconds.
6. Transfer the mayonnaise to an airtight container and refrigerate.

Spices
Portuguese Dry Rub

Next time you want to add a great flavor to fish, chicken, beef, pork and more, look no further than this recipe for a flavorful homemade dry rub.

Ingredients:
2 ½ tablespoons of paprika
2 tablespoons salt
2 tablespoons garlic powder
1 tablespoon ground black pepper
1 tablespoon onion powder
1 tablespoon cayenne pepper
½ teaspoon of turmeric

Directions:
Combine all ingredients in a large bowl and mix well. Store in an airtight container or an empty spice container.

NOTES:

15875333R00071

Printed in Great Britain
by Amazon